Ecology

Interactions in the Biosphere

Author: Debbie Routh
Consultant: Schyrlet Cameron
Editor: Mary Dieterich
Proofreaders: Margaret Brown and Alexis Fey

ISBN 978-1-62223-892-7

Printing No. CD-405085

Mark Twain Media, Inc., Publishers
Distributed by Carson Dellosa Education

Table of Contents

Introduction

Welcome, student observers, to some amazing Earth facts. In this unit, you will learn what you can do to make a difference in your environment and help protect the future of Earth. Topics covered in this unit include air, water, and land pollution and their effects. You will explore environmental topics including acid rain, the greenhouse effect, and biomes, and you will reflect on population studies.

Each environment has its own unique characteristics. You will learn about the various factors that determine each environment. The **organisms** (living things) that live in each area of our diverse biosphere are adapted or well suited to live in each of these areas.

You will learn about biotic and abiotic factors and their importance to life on earth. **Biotic factors** are the living parts of an environment. These are things like plants, animals, and other organisms in the area. **Abiotic factors** shape global and regional climates—these include physical factors, such as temperature, light, water, and soil.

Student observers, you will use many science process skills to discover the influence humans have on the environment. This book on **habitats** (the places where living things live), **niches** (the role organisms play within their habitats), and **food chains** (the interdependence of organisms—predators and prey) makes this important natural science called ecology come alive.

Teacher Note: This book supports the National Science Education Standards and is designed to supplement your existing science curriculum or to be taught as a thematic unit on ecology. Each lesson opens with a manageable amount of text for the student to read. The succeeding pages contain exercises and illustrations that are varied and plentiful. The lessons may be used as a complete unit for the entire class or as a supplement for the reluctant learner. The tone of the book is informal; a dialogue is established between the book and the student. Use this book to keep your students informed of local and global issues affecting the environment. Get your students involved in community projects, whether it is recycling, tree planting, or educating others about the dangers to our environment.

What Is Ecology?

Ecology (ee-KAHL-uh-jee) is the study of living things in their **environment** (in-VY-run-munt), or natural surroundings. This is everything **biotic** (living) and **abiotic** (nonliving) that is around them. All living things are affected by their environment and have an effect on their environment. The word *ecology* came from the Greek word *okologie*, meaning the study of homes and estates. This refers to the home or surroundings in which an **organism** (living thing) lives. A German naturalist, Ernst H. Haeckel, was the first person to use the term ecology in its present meaning. An **ecologist** is a scientist who studies the relationships between living things and their environment. An ecologist investigates how plants and animals, including people, live with and affect each other and their surroundings.

The Biosphere

The part of the earth that supports life is called the **biosphere**. The top portion of the earth's crust, all the water on the earth's surface, and the surrounding atmosphere make up the very thin layer called the biosphere. All the different environments that are home to different kinds of organisms are found in the biosphere.

Importance

All living things need materials to carry out their life processes. These materials come from the environment. Organisms get nutrients, water, oxygen, carbon dioxide, and energy from their environments. **Nutrients** (NOO-tree-unts) are used for growth, repair, and energy. Plants get their nutrients and water from the soil. Plants take in carbon dioxide from the air. They obtain energy directly from the sun. Sunlight is the source of energy that fuels most life on Earth. They then use sunlight and carbon dioxide to make food for energy. Animals get nutrients and energy by eating plants. Some animals also obtain energy by eating other animals. Many animals get their oxygen from the air. Aquatic animals with gills get their oxygen from the water. Water is a key component allowing organisms to process these materials from the environment. All living things need and use water.

Interactions

Start with any **habitat** (natural home) of an organism. The group of animals and plants that live there make up a **community**. Lift up a stone, and you will most likely find a spider, centipede, woodlouse, or earthworm. These are all a part of the stone habitat. Together, they make a community. The stone may lie next to a pond and become a part of the pond community. The pond may be in a forest and be part of the woodland community. Smaller habitats are usually a part of bigger habitats. A different community lives in each larger habitat. The organisms interact or act upon each other and the nonliving parts of the environment. Waste that is produced by the animals enriches the soil. This helps the plants grow and thrive in the community. As you see, observers, everything is connected and stretches into a vast web. When the community is healthy, it is stable and balanced. You can try to find some different habitats in your area. Be sure to look everywhere, and leave everything the way you found it.

Name: ______________________________ Date: ______________

What Is Ecology?: Reinforcement Activity

To the student observer: Can you list some ways you affect your environment?

____

____

____

Analyze: Can you identify the various environments that make up your everyday life?

____

____

____

Completion: Write the term that best completes each statement in the space provided.

environment	**materials**	**community**	**ecology**	**habitat**	**biosphere**
carbon dioxide	**nutrients**	**abiotic**	**biotic**	**interact**	**plants**

1. The study of living things and their environment is ____________________.
2. Everything that surrounds a living thing makes up its ____________________.
3. Living things get the ____________________ they need to survive from their environment.
4. Animals get their energy by eating ____________________ and other animals.
5. Plants use sunlight and ____________________ to grow and make food.
6. Living things use materials called ____________________ for growth and energy.
7. All living things act upon, or ____________________ with, their environments.
8. The ____________________ factors are the living things in the environment.
9. The ____________________ factors are the nonliving things in the environment.
10. The part of the earth that supports life is the ____________________.
11. A ____________________ is the natural home of an organism.
12. All the organisms that live in an area make up a ____________________.

Think About It:
Can you list five things all living things get from their environments?

1. ____________________ 2. ____________________

3. ____________________ 4. ____________________

5. ____________________

What Is an Ecosystem?

An **ecosystem** consists of a given habitat and its community. A community is all the populations living in a certain place. A population is all of the same kind of organisms living in that certain place. The living (**biotic**) and nonliving (**abiotic**) things in an environment together with their interactions make up the ecosystem. The habitat and all the interactions going on inside form a self-contained ecological unit.

Populations

A **population** is all of the same kind of organism living in a certain place. Different populations may live in the same environment. Study or visualize a pond near your home. Are there different organisms that live in the pond? Do you see frogs and toads? Maybe you see a few cattails, some fish, and overhead you hear ducks as they come in for a fantastic landing. There are 5 toads, 10 frogs, 20 minnows, 15 catfish, 10 blue gill, 6 ducks, and a lot of cattails. The five toads make up one population within the community. The 15 catfish make up another population in the community. What is the duck population of the pond community? If you could get a microscope and a drop of the pond water, you would see many other **microorganisms** (tiny living things) living in the pond community.

Communities

All the different populations living together and reacting in the habitat make up a unique **community**. Organisms interact with each other and the other things in the environment. There are many kinds and sizes of ecosystems. A rotting log, puddle of water, or even something as big as a desert can be an ecosystem. All ecosystems must be able to support all the organisms that live in or on that habitat. To support organisms, these four processes must occur:

1. The production of energy is one process that must occur inside the community. The sun is a source of energy in most ecosystems.
2. Energy must be transferred to plants that make their own food. The stored energy then is passed on to animals when they eat the plants.
3. When organisms die, they must decay, or break down, so that other living things can reuse these **nutrients** (raw materials).
4. This decomposition of dead materials is then recycled. As the materials break down, they return to the soil and are reused over and over.

What Is an Ecosystem? (cont.)

Habitats

A **habitat** is where an organism lives. The habitat provides everything an organism needs in order to survive. It has the food and water supply necessary to live. It also provides suitable shelter and a place to reproduce. As we said earlier, it may be very large or very small. There are water habitats and land habitats. The entire ocean is the habitat for whales. A habitat for a woodpecker may be as small as one tree in the forest. Even an anthill is a habitat.

Niches

Every organism has a certain role or job they perform within the community. What is your role or job right now? Did you answer "a student"? That is the job you have right now where you live. The job each organism fills within the community is its **niche** (NITCH or NEESH). This includes everything the organism does or needs.

Since many kinds of organisms share the same habitat, they must have certain roles within the community so that everything stays balanced. Each performs a different role and has different needs so the habitat can support everything living there. Wolves and elk share the same habitat, but they do not have the same niche. They do not eat the same thing or require the same shelter. If they did, they would not be able to live together for very long. One would be able to do the job better and end up crowding out the other one. What would happen if the elk and the wolves ate the same food? There might not be enough for both, and one would eventually perform the job better and take over the food supply. The other population would need to leave and find a new habitat or end up starving. If two populations shared the same niche, the one best suited to the role would survive and reproduce. Two populations may share the same habitat, but they cannot share the same niche.

Name: ______________________________ Date: ______________

What Is An Ecosystem?: Reinforcement Activity

To the student observer: Study the image on page 5, and see if you can identify the community.

The image represents a ______________ community.

Analyze: Observe the image again and see if you can identify the largest population in number and the smallest population in number. What other populations might exist there?

Largest: ______________ Smallest: ______________

Other: ______________________________

Completion:

1. A ______________ is all the different kinds of organisms that live in a certain place.
2. All the biotic and abiotic things in an environment and their interactions make up an ______________.
3. The ______________ is the main source of energy in most ecosystems.
4. When an organism dies, its body ______________, or breaks down.
5. The anthill is the ______________ for the ants in your backyard.
6. The role of an organism in the habitat is its ______________.
7. Two populations may share the same ______________ but not the same ______________.
8. All ecosystems must be self-supporting. Can you identify the four processes that occur in an ecosystem?

   a. ______________ b. ______________

   c. ______________ d. ______________

Making an Inference: Polar bears live in a cold, arctic habitat. Could this animal live in a hot, dry desert? Why or why not?

____

____

____

Learning About the Web of Life

Algae floating on top of a pond capture the energy from the sun. The algae use this energy to create sugar (food) and other molecules. A small fish eats the algae, and then a bigger fish eats the small fish. A bird then swoops down and eats the bigger fish. This is the beginning of a feeding order called a food chain. A **food chain** is the feeding order of organisms in a community.

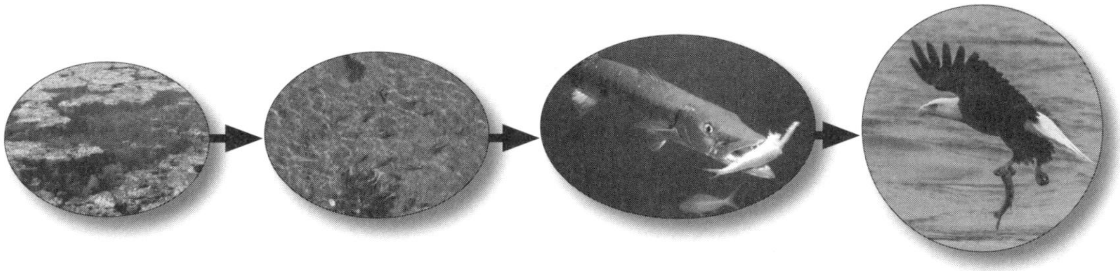

All food chains begin with plants or other organisms that can collect energy from sunlight. These organisms that capture the energy from the sun are called **producers**.

Producers

Plants, some protists, and some kinds of bacteria are all producers. These organisms can make or produce their own food. Every food chain begins with a producer. Producers use sunlight to make their food by a process called **photosynthesis**.

Consumers

Any organism that cannot make its own food through photosynthesis must obtain its food from outside its body. **Consumers** get their food by eating, or consuming, other organisms. All animals and fungi, as well as some protists and bacteria, are consumers.

Consumers may eat plants or other consumers. Consumers that eat only plants, such as rabbits, are **herbivores**. Consumers that eat other animals, such as wolves, are **carnivores**. Some consumers, such as bears, are omnivores. **Omnivores** eat both plants and animals.

Consumers in a food chain are classified into different feeding levels, called **orders**, depending on what they consume. **First-order consumers** eat plants, **second-order consumers** eat animals that eat plants, and **third-order consumers** eat animals that eat other animals. In one such food chain, a rabbit (first-order consumer) eats grasses, a snake (second-order consumer) eats the rabbit, and a hawk (third-order consumer) eats the snake.

Pyramid of Producers and Consumers

You might also think of a food chain as a pyramid. The plains are covered with various species of grass plants. This makes plenty of food for the herds of antelope to feed on. The number of antelope is less than the number of grass plants. In the same area there may be a few dozen mountain lions. Lions need a wide range in which to hunt. The food chain pyramid has the highest-level consumers at the top. Each time you go up the pyramid, the original source of energy that was trapped by the plants decreases each time the energy is passed on to the next order of consumers. As a result, the size of the population decreases.

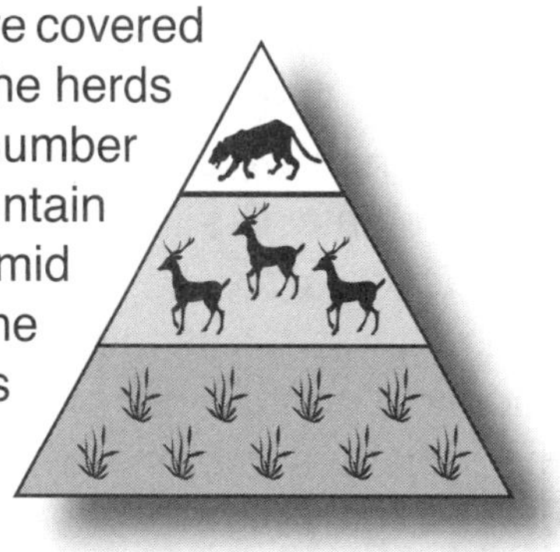

Learning About the Web of Life (cont.)

Food Webs

Most consumers eat more than one kind of food. Eating a variety of foods helps ensure the survival of the organism by providing a sufficient food supply. Within a pond community, the frog eats a variety of foods, including insects and worms. Both snakes and birds then eat the frogs. Frogs become part of two different food chains, with each food chain linked together at certain points. All the food chains in the community that are linked together become a **food web**.

Decomposers

What happens when a high-level consumer, such as a mountain lion, dies? Do you think the food chain stops there? No, **decomposers** continue the food chain by feeding on the dead animal. Decomposers get their food by breaking down complex chemicals in dead organisms into simple chemicals that become part of the soil. Decomposers can be bacteria, fungi, and some protists. They feed on producers and consumers at each level of the pyramid. Plants take in the chemicals from the soil through their roots and use them to grow. Over time, these chemicals are used over and over again by plants, transferred to herbivores and carnivores, and returned to the soil by decomposers. The chemical's location and form change, but the amount of the chemical stays the same.

Flow of Energy

You and other organisms need energy to live. Your muscles use energy as you work. Sometimes, you may feel like you have "run out of energy." If so, you take a break and eat some food to replenish your energy supply. Food contains chemical energy that was produced during photosynthesis. During photosynthesis, light energy is converted to chemical energy that is stored in the sugar molecules. As plant cells break down nutrients, the stored energy is released. The energy is used for their life processes. As plants use this energy, some is changed to heat. The heat becomes part of the environment. The rest of the energy is stored in the plants' tissues. When you eat foods, such as potatoes and other vegetables, you take in the plants' stored chemical energy. Each time the energy stored in plants is passed on from one organism to another, some of the energy is used up or lost as heat. The rest is stored as chemical energy in the nutrients of the organism's body. Each time the energy is passed up the food chain, some energy is lost as heat, some is used for life processes, and the rest is stored in the organism.

Name: ______________________ Date: ______________

Learning About the Web of Life: Reinforcement Activity

To the student observer: Do you know the difference between a consumer and a producer? Explain.

____

____

Analyze: What kind of consumer are you when you eat a cheeseburger with the works? Explain or diagram the different food chains you are a part of when you eat your sandwich.

____

____

Completion:

1. Producers use energy from the ______________ to make their own food.
2. Food chains always begin with a ______________.
3. ______________ are organisms that break down the remains of dead animals.
4. ______________ are producers in lakes and oceans.
5. Organisms that eat only producers are ______________-order consumers.
6. Consumers get food by ______________ other organisms.

Identify:

Classify the organisms below as A. herbivores, B. carnivores, or C. omnivores.

1. ______ Bear	2. ______ Hawk	3. ______ Horse
4. ______ Giraffe	5. ______ Human	6. ______ Wolf

Prove You Can:

1. On your own paper, diagram a food chain that includes three levels or orders of consumers. Which order (level) of consumer has the smallest population size?
2. Explain the relationship between food chains and food webs. ______________

   ____
3. Why is less energy available at each higher level of a food chain?

   ____

   ____

   ____
4. What is the role of decomposers in the community? ______________

   ____

Name: ______________________________ Date: ________________

Symbiosis

Ecosystems are very delicate and must maintain a natural balance. Organisms maintain this natural balance through **symbiosis** (relationships between two organisms). There are three different types of symbiosis.

Types of Symbiosis

Name	Definition	Example
Mutualism	- both organisms benefit	- flower and bee
Commensalism	- one organism benefits - the other is unaffected	- monarch butterfly and milkweed plant
Parasitism	- one organism benefits - the other is harmed	- tick and dog

Symbiosis: Reinforcement Activity

Directions: Complete the graphic organizer with examples of each type of symbiotic relationship.

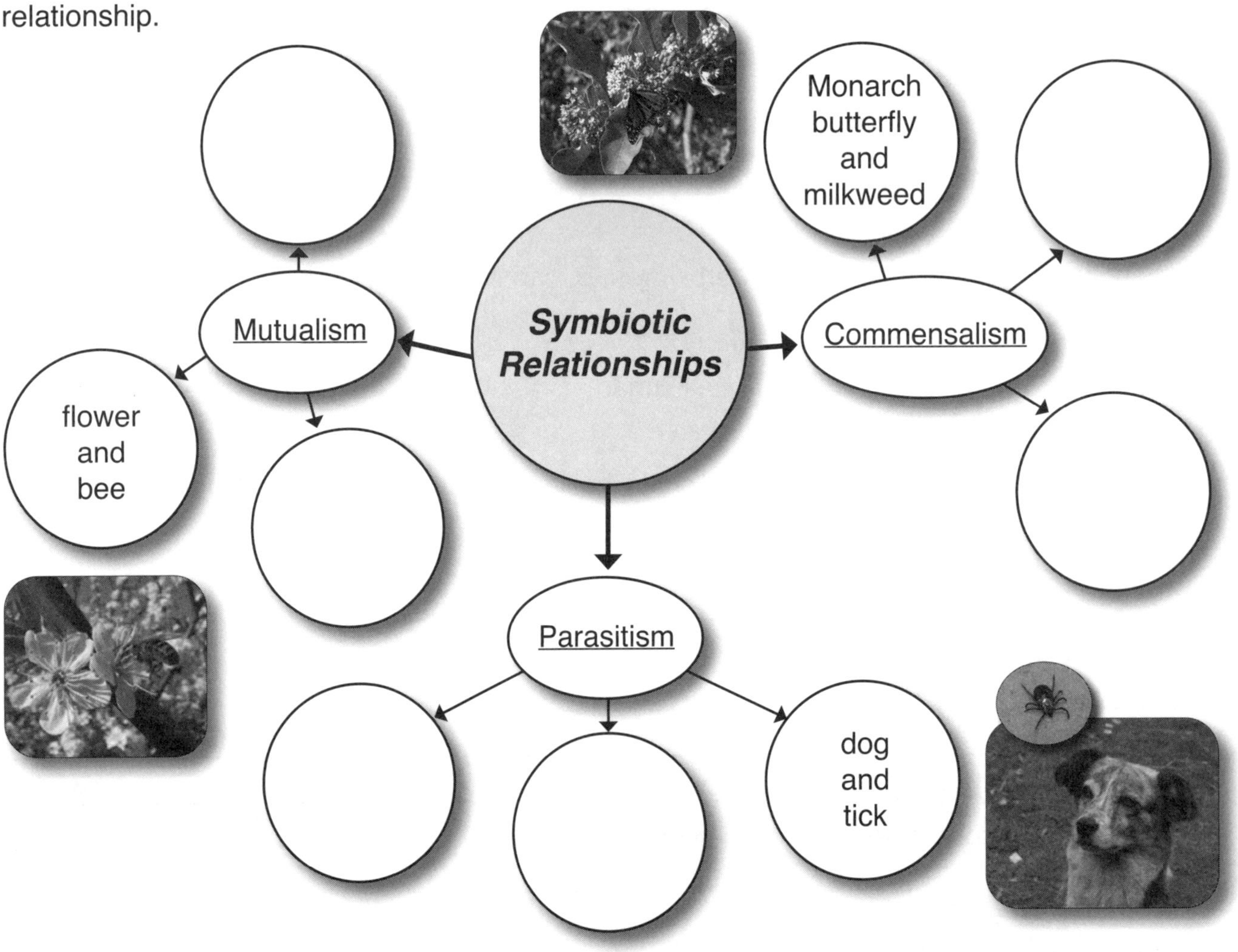

Name: ______________________________ Date: ______________

Predator and Prey Adaptations

Predators are animals that hunt other animals for food. **Prey** are the animals that are hunted. When the chase is on, each animal has certain adaptations that give it an advantage. Adaptations come in many forms that range from simple coloring to complex body parts.

Predator Adaptations	Prey Adaptations
- good sense of smell - specialized teeth - intelligence (larger brain) - camouflage: color, stripes, spots - larger size - claws or talons - specialized tongues - speed - venom	- swivel ears - speed - antlers or horns - larger feet - armor or quills - stings - tusks - odor - camouflage: color, stripes, spots

Predator and Prey Adaptations: Reinforcement Activity

Directions: Complete the chart by filling in the columns with at least three animals that have the adaptation listed for that column.

Predator and Prey Adaptations				
claws or talons	**specialized teeth**	**stingers**	**camouflage**	**horns or antlers**

Round and Round We Go: Cycles in the Ecosystem

There are many cycles in nature. A **cycle** is something that happens over and over again in the same way. The earth is sometimes compared to a spaceship. The planet Earth is isolated in space like a spaceship. All the materials we need to build our homes, to make our tools, and to grow the food we eat come from the biosphere. Materials in the biosphere must be used over and over again. The materials we need to live must be continuously cycled between the living and the nonliving parts of the earth. If a material is in short supply, we may not be able to get more of it. Rocks move through a cycle changing from one kind of rock to another. Chemicals important to life are also cycled through the environment. Some cycles important to life are water, carbon dioxide, oxygen, and nitrogen.

The Water Cycle

Water falls to the earth as **precipitation**, or rain, snow, sleet, and hail. The most noticeable water in the ecosystem is in lakes, rivers, and the ocean. There is also **groundwater**, or water just beneath the surface of the land. What happens when a puddle dries up? The liquid water changes to a gas, or **evaporates**, forming **water vapor**. **Evaporation** is the water vapor that rises from oceans, rivers, and lakes and becomes part of the air. Organisms produce water as they get energy from the food they eat through cellular respiration. Plants release water vapor from their leaves. Animals release water vapor with their breath and liquid water with their wastes. Water vapor is always in the air, but you cannot see it.

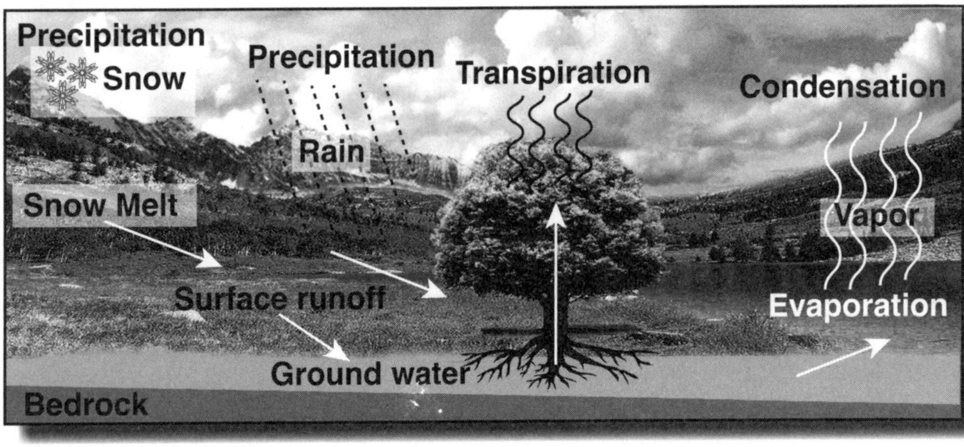

Have you ever noticed how the outside of your glass of ice water becomes wet? The water vapor in the air **condenses**, or changes into a liquid, on the outside of the glass. This happens when the air next to the glass cools from the ice and condenses. **Condensation** occurs as water vapor in the air cools and condenses into water droplets in the clouds. When enough water gathers in the clouds, precipitation falls in the form of rain, snow, sleet, or hail. The water is returned to the earth to be reused by organisms.

Water is essential for life, making up 75% of all organisms. Organisms need water for various life processes. Water is cycled by falling as a liquid, evaporating as a gas, and then cooling enough to become a liquid again. Water is continuously recycled between the bodies of water, air, and land, creating suitable conditions for life to exist.

Round and Round We Go: Cycles in the Ecosystem (cont.)

The Oxygen-Carbon Dioxide Cycle

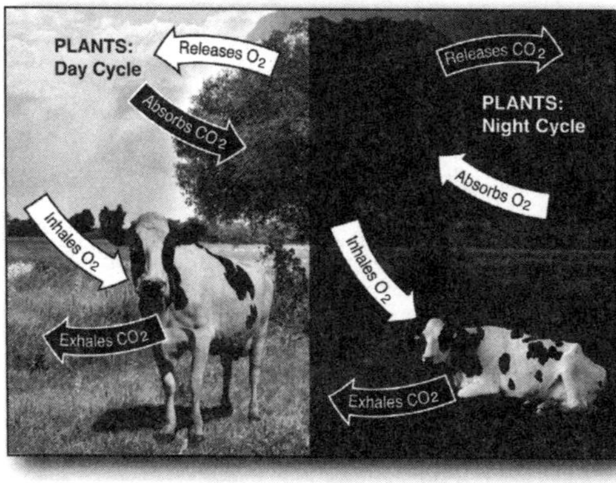

Like water, oxygen and carbon dioxide also cycle through the ecosystem. All living things are made up of the life substance **carbon**. Chemicals that contain carbon are carbohydrates, fats, and proteins. Carbon can also be found in the nonliving parts of the environment. Carbon dioxide gas is in the air, bodies of water, and fossil fuels such as coal and oil.

Oxygen is a gas that is essential to almost every life form. Oxygen is also found in air and bodies of water. Most of the oxygen that organisms use comes from producers (plants). The oxygen is used to release energy that is stored in food.

During **photosynthesis**, plants use (take in) carbon dioxide to make food and give off oxygen as a waste product. During **respiration**, animals use or take in oxygen and give off carbon dioxide as waste. During cellular respiration, plants and other organisms produce carbon dioxide. **Decomposers** release carbon dioxide as they break down dead organisms. People release carbon dioxide when they burn fossil fuels. As you can see, through respiration and photosynthesis, carbon dioxide and oxygen are continuously recycled in our ecosystems.

Nitrogen Cycle

Nitrogen is a gas that makes up 78% of the air. All living things need nitrogen to make proteins. Unfortunately, the most abundant gas in the atmosphere cannot be used in its natural form. It is used and reused in the atmosphere with the help of a certain kind of bacteria. These nitrogen-fixing bacteria live in the soil and in the roots of some plants. **Nitrogen-fixing bacteria** change nitrogen gas into nitrogen compounds, or **nitrates**. Plants take in the nitrates through their roots and use it to make chemicals they need.

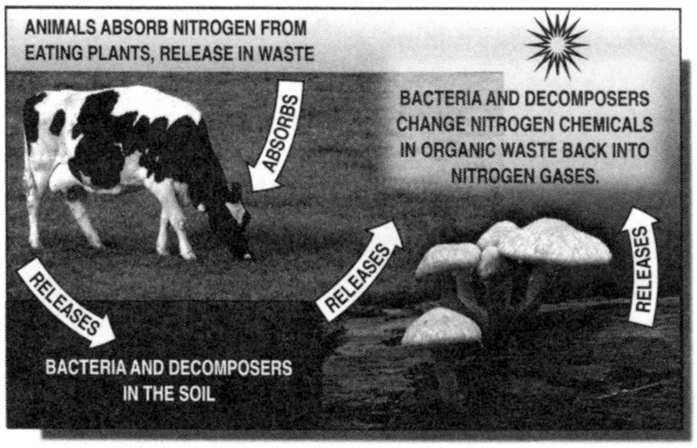

Animals get the nitrogen they need by eating plants. Some kinds of bacteria will change any nitrates not used by the plant back to nitrogen gases. When an organism dies, decomposers will also change the nitrogen chemicals found in the organism back into nitrogen gases. The nitrogen cycle continues as the nitrogen gases are released back into the air.

System of Cycles

Cycles in an ecosystem are linked to one another by photosynthesis and cellular respiration. Plants take in carbon dioxide (CO_2) and water (H_2O) for photosynthesis and release oxygen (O_2). Animals and plants use O_2 for cellular respiration and release CO_2 and H_2O. Scientists may study one cycle at a time to make it easier for them to understand what is happening independently. However, each cycle is only a small part of the system of cycles that interact with one another.

Name: ______________________________ Date: ______________

Cycles in the Ecosystem: Reinforcement Activity

To the student observer: Do you know what four substances are recycled continuously?

____

____

Analyze: Can you explain why certain materials must be cycled in our environment?

____

____

____

Completion:

1. During ____________________, plants use carbon dioxide from the air.
2. All organisms need nitrogen to make ____________________.
3. ____________________ change nitrogen into a form that can be used by plants.
4. The ____________________ we need must be cycled continuously.
5. During photosynthesis, plants use carbon dioxide and release ____________________ as waste.
6. Water is cycled through the environment by falling as a ____________________ and then ____________________ as a gas.
7. ____________________ and ____________________ are cycled through the environment by photosynthesis and respiration.
8. During respiration, animals use oxygen and release ____________________ as waste.
9. Animals get the nitrogen they need by eating ____________________.

Predict:
If all the plants on Earth began to die, what would happen to the oxygen content of the air?

____

____

Name That Cycle: Study the illustrations below and properly identify them.

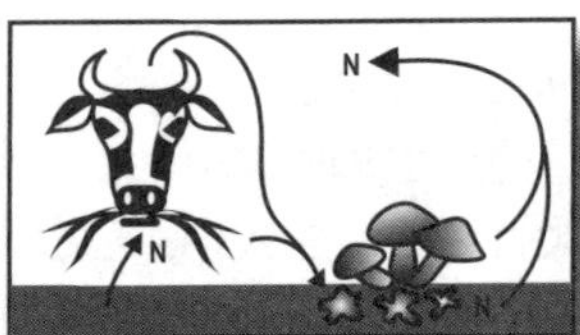

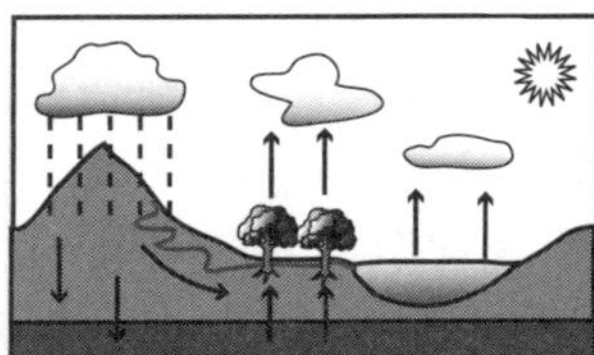

a. ____________________ b. ____________________ c. ____________________

What Are Biomes?

Regions of the Earth

The earth can be divided into large regions called **biomes.** Each biome has its own kind of climate, soil, plants, and animals. There are six major land biomes and two major aquatic biomes, as well as other smaller biomes, as you can see from the map below. The weather in an area over a long period of time is the area's **climate**. Each biome has a different climate. Climate helps to determine what kind of plants and animals can live in that area. The types of organisms found in a biome depend on the resources available to the organisms. **Resources** are the things organisms use to live. This is why you will never find a cactus growing in the rain forest—too much water.

Living in the Tundra

The **tundra** is a climate with very harsh winters, a low average temperature, little moisture, and a short summer season. There are two kinds of tundra: **arctic tundra** and **alpine tundra**. Arctic tundra is found in the arctic areas of the world near the poles and is influenced by **permafrost**, which is permanently frozen ground. Alpine tundra is found on mountains at an altitude above the tree line.

Mosses, lichens, grasses, small wild flowers, and shrubs are the only plants that can survive in the tundra. Because the growing season is so short, these plants reproduce by division and budding instead of by flower pollination.

Animal life in the arctic tundra includes the arctic hare, arctic fox, musk ox, lemming, caribou, and snowy owl. The alpine tundra includes the big horn sheep, foxes, marmots, and mountain goats.

Living in the Taiga

The **taiga** biome is another cold biome, stretching across the northern portions of North America, Europe, and Asia close to the tundra. There is a wide range of temperatures between winter and summer seasons. The winters are long and cold, and the summers are short and cool. Precipitation is moderately high throughout the year, with snow occurring during the winter months. Most of the taiga in North America was once covered with glaciers that have receded, leaving gouges and depressions in the topography. Since there is moderately high

What Are Biomes? (cont.)

precipitation, these gouges and depressions are frequently filled with water, creating bogs and lakes.

The soil found in the taiga is high in acid. The main plant life is **conifers**, trees that have cones and needle-like leaves. These are evergreens such as spruce, fir, and pine. Under certain conditions, broadleaf trees, such as birch and aspen, are able to survive the harsh climate of the taiga. This area is our main source of lumber.

The cold climate of the taiga prevents many animals from living there year-round. Some of the large animals found in the taiga include moose, deer, and wolves. Examples of smaller animals that live in the taiga are lynx, squirrels, and weasels. Because this northern region, just south of the tundra, is dominated by cone-bearing trees, it is sometimes referred to as the coniferous forest biome.

Living in the Temperate Deciduous Forest

Deciduous forests can be found in the eastern half of North America, the middle of Europe, and eastern Asia. This region has a moderate climate, a long growing season, and cold winters. All four seasons visit this biome.

The area is home to many different species of plants and animals. Deciduous trees that have leaves that turn various colors and fall off each autumn dominate this area. The leaves are broad, flat leaves that fall to the ground and decay as the tree becomes dormant in winter.

Many kinds of birds and animals live in the deciduous forest biome for three seasons and then hibernate or migrate during the winter. Squirrels, deer, raccoons, skunks, hawks, and cardinals, to name just a few, live in the deciduous forests. This is a region that is losing ground at an alarming rate to development. These animals are losing their homes.

Living in the Tropical Rain Forests

The **tropical rain forest** climate is found near the equator. It is warm and humid throughout the year. It has very warm days with beautiful mornings full of sunshine. Late afternoon brings thunderstorms with heavy rainfall. The average annual rainfall totals 80–100 inches or more.

Many kinds of plants grow well in the tropical rain forest. Tall trees form a canopy that blocks out the sunlight, making the forest floor dark. Few plants grow on the forest floor. Many plants in this region grow on other plants. Since they grow on the surface of other plants, they do not have roots. Plants that do have roots climb or vine up the trees so the leaves can reach sunlight.

Many large and small animals are at home in the rain forest. Jaguars, pumas, snakes, birds, and monkeys are only a few. Many of the animals spend most of their lives in the trees. They hunt, eat, and sleep in the forest canopy. This is another region that is shrinking in size. Plants and animals are endangered because large numbers of trees are being cut down for lumber. As the forest becomes smaller, there is less food and living space for the animals.

What Are Biomes? (cont.)

Living in the Grasslands

Grassland biomes can be found in the middle latitudes in the interiors of continents. A grassland is a region where the average annual precipitation is great enough to support grasses and, in some areas, a few trees. In temperate grasslands, the average rainfall per year ranges from 10–30 inches. In tropical and sub-tropical grasslands, the average rainfall per year ranges from 25–60 inches per year. Grasslands are sometimes called prairies and are more than just dry, flat areas. The prairies contain many different species of plants and animals.

The most common types of plant life on the North American prairie are grasses, sunflowers, asters, coneflowers, and clover. This is the biome where large herds of animals live. Some common animals in the grasslands are bison, coyotes, eagles, bobcats, wild turkey, Canadian geese, and crickets.

Living in the Desert

Deserts cover about one fifth of the land and can be hot or cold. Most **hot deserts** are near the Tropic of Cancer or the Tropic of Capricorn. They are sandy and rocky, receiving little rain. The average temperature ranges from 20° to 25° C. The extreme maximum temperature for hot deserts ranges from 43.5° to 49° C. The **cold deserts** are near the arctic parts of the world. The cold deserts' average temperature in winter ranges from -2° to 4° C and in the summer 21° to 26° C. Cold deserts usually have plenty of snow and ice, but their temperatures are so cold that almost all forms of life are unable to survive.

Few plants and animals can survive in the desert regions of the world. In the hot deserts, plants are almost all ground-hugging shrubs, short woody trees, or cacti. All of these plants are packed with nutrients and can handle hot weather by storing water for long periods of time. The only plants that can survive in a cold desert are algae that live in frozen lakes.

Hot desert animals include mostly **nocturnal** (only active at night) animals, such as foxes, lizards, kangaroo rats, and snakes. The only animals that survive in cold deserts depend on the oceans that surround the icy land. Animals like seals, polar bears near the North Pole, and penguins near the South Pole may rest on the land, but eat the products of the oceans.

Living in Water

Most of the earth's surface is water. Water can be **salt water**, which includes the oceans and the seas. This is also called the marine biome. Water can also be **freshwater**, which does not contain salt, and includes lakes, streams, rivers, and ponds. Some water is **brackish**, which is where the two **merge**, or join, and it is slightly salty. These areas are called **estuaries**. Aquatic biomes are home to many plants and animals.

Saltwater animals range from mammals, like dolphins, to bony fish, such as clown fish, to cartilaginous fish, such as sharks, and others. Freshwater animals include mammals, like otters, bony fish, such as piranhas, and more. Some animals can survive in both salt and freshwater. Animals such as eels and salmon are born in one type of water, migrate to the other to live, and return to their birthplace to start the cycle over.

Name: ______________________ Date: ______________

What Are Biomes?: Reinforcement Activity

To the student observer: Explain what a biome is.

Analyze: Identify the biome in which you live.

Identify:

1. Which biome is the coldest biome? ______________
2. Which biome is the driest biome? ______________
3. Which biome is hot and wet? ______________
4. Which biome is home to large numbers of grazing animals? ______________
5. In which biome would you find a shark living? ______________

Compare and Contrast:

Deserts and the rain forests are both located in hot areas. The tundra and the taiga are both located in cold areas. Choose one of these pairs, and detail how they are the same and how they are different. Use the T-chart at the right to organize your ideas.

Lake Victoria and the Miracle Fish: Introduction of a New Species

In this lesson, you will learn about making difficult decisions about complex issues. You will discover these issues usually involve a **trade-off** (giving up one thing in favor of another). This story will introduce you to a key ecological concept involving the introduction of non-native species to an environment. You will soon realize that introducing a new species to an environment can have both intended and unintended consequences for the ecosystem. As you read the scenario and story below, decide for yourself if the Nile perch is truly a miracle fish.

The Scenario:

A teenage boy of Kenya sits outside his hut. Inside, his mother is preparing the evening meal. Nearby, his sister and brother lay out the afternoon catch to dry in the sun. The young man begins to visit with you about the family's fishing boat and then begins his story. He says, "My father was one of the best fishermen in our village. He still catches all kinds of fish, though it is much harder than it used to be. Most of the fish in the lake used to be very small—two to four inches long. It was easy for him to catch hundreds of fish in his net. About the time my sister was born, the number of small fish my father could catch in his net began to go way down. Luckily, our government introduced a new fish into the lake. Now, the most common fish in the lake is a much larger fish—the Nile perch. It is too heavy for us to catch with a net in our small boat. That's why my father now works for one of the fishing companies. They have very big boats to catch the Nile perch. I work there too—I earn money to help feed my family."

The Story:

Lake Victoria is the second-largest lake in the world. Three countries surround it: Tanzania, Uganda, and Kenya. Tanzania controls 51%, Uganda controls 43% and Kenya controls just 6% of this large but shallow lake. It contains some very large fish, the Nile perch, some weighing over 240 kilograms (529 pounds). However, the average Nile perch weighs 6–9 kilograms (7–13 pounds).

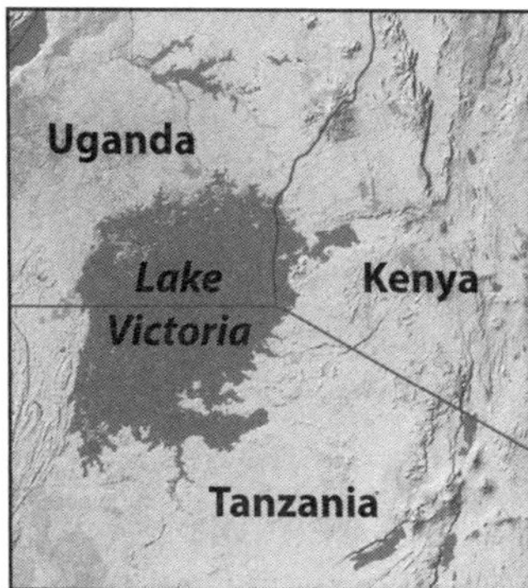

Many families relied on the lake for food. Until the 1980s, the lake's most common fish were cichlids (SICK-lids), a small freshwater fish. Have you seen oscars or angelfish in an aquarium? If so, you've seen a cichlid. Since the fish were small, they could easily be caught with simple nets and a canoe. Cichlids are interesting to ecologists because there are so many different species of cichlids. Ecologists believed over 300 different species of cichlids lived in the lake—most of these could not be found anywhere else in the world.

The Problem:

By the 1950s, the lake was showing signs of being overfished—too few fish were left. With such low population numbers, they could not reproduce. This could eventually lead to a lack of food for the villagers to eat and sell.

Lake Victoria and the Miracle Fish (cont.)

What Was Done:

During the 1950s, government leaders decided to introduce a new species to increase the amount of fish available to feed the villagers and to sell to other countries. Ecologists worried about this decision because this new species, the Nile perch, would not have any **predators** (natural enemies) in the lake. They predicted it would have a negative effect on the ecosystem. Nile perch were secretly added to the lake before a decision was made. In the early 1960s, more Nile perch were added deliberately by government officials.

The Outcome:

In the 1960s, 100,000 metric tons of fish, including cichlids, were caught each year in Lake Victoria. By the 1990s, the fishing companies were removing nearly 500,000 metric tons of fish from the lake. The graph at the right shows only Kenya's share of the fish for 1980 to 1995. Study the data in the graph to see how the amount of fish caught by Kenyan fisheries changed over a 15-year period. Predict what you think the outcome was after 1995 from the decision to introduce Nile perch to the lake.

Amount of Fish Caught in Lake Victoria by Kenyan Fisheries

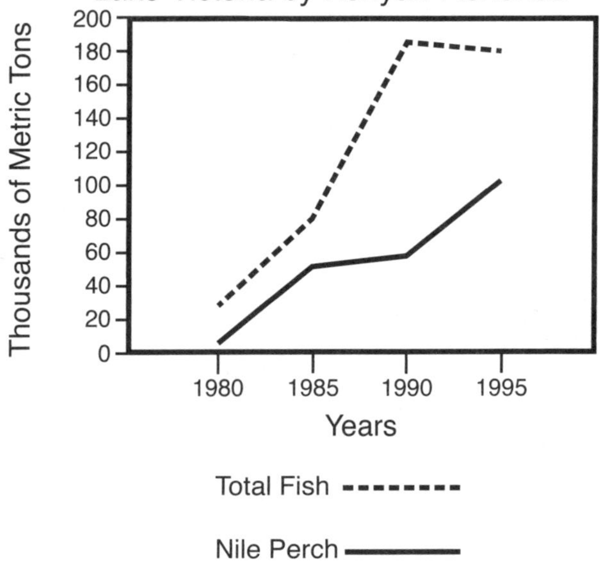

The Nile perch is believed to have caused the extinction of 200 species of cichlids. Other fish populations are also declining. Some of the cichlids ate algae. With their numbers falling, the algae has greatly increased in population. Algae use up the oxygen in the lake, making it difficult for other aquatic organisms to survive. Today, the deepest parts of the lake are considered "dead," which means they don't contain living matter.

Think It Over:

Was the original goal met? In 1979, there were over 16,000 fishermen in Kenya alone. In 1993, the large fishing companies employed over 82,000 fishermen in the country. The Nile perch has brought in money for these African countries, and the local people who eat the fish call it a miracle. Ecologists wonder how long this will last. The Nile perch are the top predators in the lake. What will happen when their food supply, the other fish in the lake, is gone? Will the Nile perch population decrease, like the fish populations before it? Only time will tell.

Name: ______________________ Date: ______________

Lake Victoria and the Miracle Fish: Reinforcement Activity

To the student observer: Have you ever made a decision that involved a trade-off? What did you give up in order to get what you wanted? Was it worth it in the long run?

Analyze: Is there always a trade-off for introducing a new species to an area, or do you think there can be a situation where the introduction is completely positive?

Thinking It Over:

1. Based on the information in the reading about Lake Victoria, how did the total amount of fish caught each year change from the 1960s to the 1990s?

2. Study the graph on the previous page and draw a new graph on your own paper that indicates what you think happened from 1995 to the present and what you predict for the future of the fishing industry in Kenya and the other countries. Explain your reasoning.

3. Explain how the introduction of the Nile perch affected the people who lived near Lake Victoria and the organisms that lived in the lake.

State Your Opinion:

Do you believe the Nile perch should have been introduced into Lake Victoria? Support your answer with evidence that supports your point of view. Was there a trade-off for your decision?

Is There Room for One More?: Carrying Capacity: Read and Think It Over

Learning About Carrying Capacity

In this lesson, you will be challenged to understand the term *carrying capacity*. You will be studying a hypothetical experiment conducted in a nearby lake. Through this activity, you will try to explain changes in population that have taken place. Population changes may occur due to natural changes in either the living or the nonliving factors in a community. **Carrying capacity** is defined as the maximum population (number) of a species that can be adequately supported by its environment within an ecosystem. To understand carrying capacity better, think of your family car. How many people can safely ride in the family car? Remember that fluctuation of population numbers is natural to a degree. What are some factors that change populations to a level to be concerned with? Do these factors change over time?

This activity will introduce you to a career in ecology as a field biologist. You will need to decide whether a decline in population indicates trouble for a species, or if it is just a temporary, normal downward turn. The chosen species for this activity is the zebra mussel. Zebra mussel density is easy to monitor over time because the adults are stationary. You will make inferences about factors that affect the quality of water, which directly affects the mussel population. By interpreting population graphs and analyzing the effects of factors such as food supply and environmental conditions, you will determine what the carrying capacity is for a species in a habitat.

The Scenario:

You and your team of field biologists arrive at Lake Reed. About ten years ago, zebra mussels invaded Lake Reed by river. You and your team have been collecting data and carefully watching the population numbers for ten years. After a decade of study, you feel you have a good idea of how quickly the zebra mussel can populate Lake Reed. You have been keeping an ongoing count of mussels per square meter. The graph below represents the information you and your team have gathered on the mussel population.

Graph A
Mussel Population of Lake Reed

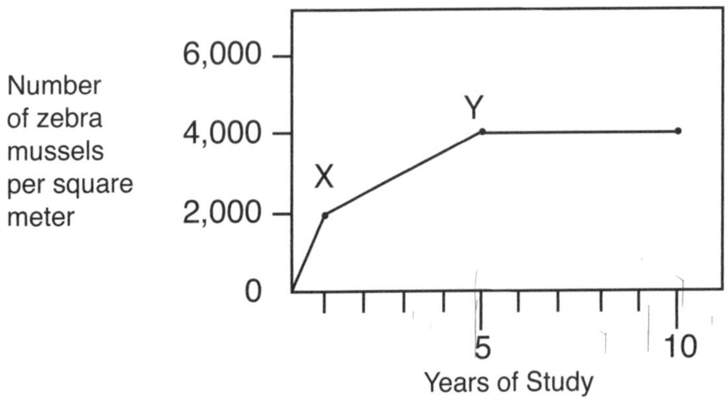

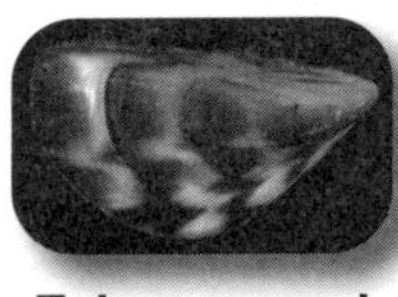

Zebra mussel

A native Great Lakes mussel encrusted with zebra mussels

Name: ______________________________ Date: ______________

Is There Room for One More? (cont.)

Your team knows that mussels obtain their food by filtering tiny organisms called plankton out of the water. Looking at the graph, you focus your attention on the quantity of plankton. Looking at points X and Y, what do you think is happening to the quantity of plankton? As you make your analysis, you think you have identified the maximum number of zebra mussels that could live successfully in Lake Reed. You are pretty sure this is the carrying capacity, or amount of mussels the lake can hold. Your team is aware that there are other factors that could affect this capacity over time. Now, study the graph again and use your knowledge to think it over below.

Thinking It Over:

1. Approximately how many mussels can the lake hold? ______________________
2. How did you determine this amount? ______________________
3. What are some factors that might affect the carrying capacity over time?

____

____

The Scenario (continued):

After completing your analysis, you and your team leave the lake. The team will return once a year and continue its study of Lake Reed. For 15 years, you and your team return faithfully to the lake and continue to collect data for each year. The information your team has collected is represented in the graph below. Analyze the data closely before you begin to think it over.

Graph B

Mussel Population of Lake Reed

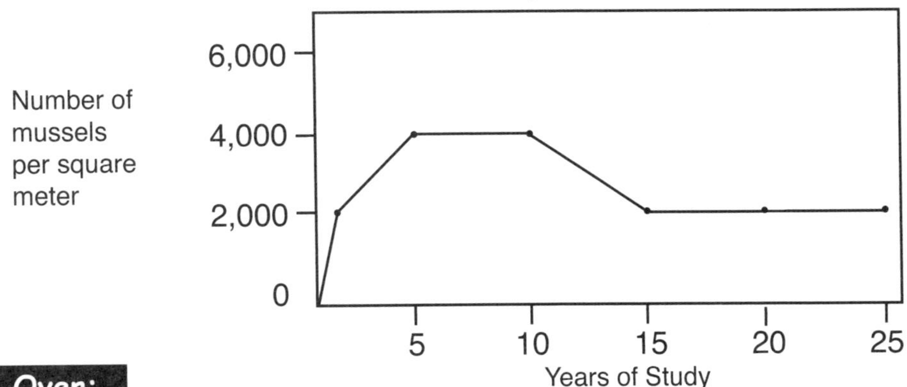

Thinking It Over:

4. What was the carrying capacity for the mussels in Lake Reed between years 15 and 25?

____

5. Identify three nonliving and three living factors that might have caused the capacity to change. Explain how each factor affected the capacity.

Nonliving Factors: ____

____

Name: ______________________________ Date: ______________

Is There Room for One More? (cont.)

Living Factors: ______________________________

____

6. Do you hypothesize the population of zebra mussels will return to the level it had reached between years 5 and 10? Why or why not? ______________________________

____

The Scenario (continued):

For years, you have been puzzled by the change in the mussel population. You have found no evidence of new predators appearing in the lake. You and your team are convinced that something has changed in the habitat to cause this shift in the population level. Then a team member, while studying public records, discovers that a new factory was built three miles up from the lake about 15 years ago. Excited about the new information, you form a hypothesis.

You decide to test your hypothesis in a controlled experiment. You decide to set up two pools for the zebra mussels to live in and a third pool for growing plankton, the mussel food source. One pool contains water from Lake Reed. The other pool contains water from a similar lake located higher in the mountains and above the factory. You add ten adult zebra mussels to each pool and begin to grow the plankton in the third pool. Each pool of mussels is supplied daily with fresh plankton. Several months later, you have found no difference at all in the mussel population of the two pools.

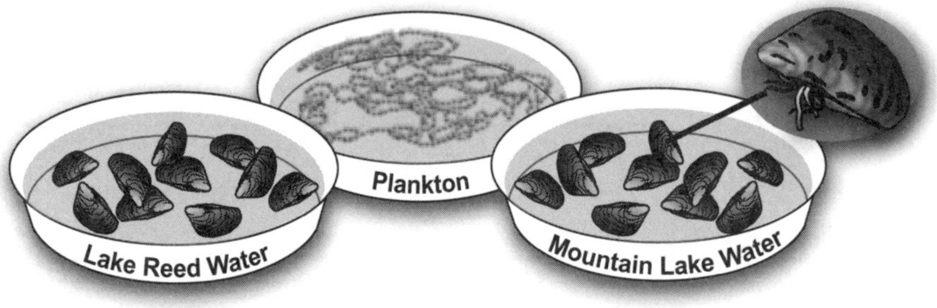

Thinking It Over:

7. What is the hypothesis? Was this a good experiment to test that hypothesis?

____

____

8. How would some different experiments designed to test this hypothesis work? Do you think you would get different results? ______________________________

____

____

Changes in Our Ecosystems

Everything changes all around us. Everything from microscopic living cells to climate and landscape are constantly changing. As communities of biotic and abiotic factors interact, they may cause changes. It may even change into a different kind of community. Some changes are very quick; others take a very long period of time to occur. The changes in our natural world that occur over time in a community are called succession. Imagine how your lawn might change if you decided not to cut the grass. First, the grass would grow taller and taller until it looked like a meadow. Later, larger plants would begin to grow, and then trees might begin to appear. **Succession** is a process in which a community gradually changes over time when the environment has changed. During the stages of succession, different plants and animals replace each other until a climax community is formed.

Succession

As an environment changes, its populations are slowly replaced by new populations. A change in one group may lead to a change in another. The first populations to change in the environment are plants. Different plants mean different first-level consumers, which in turn mean different second- and third-level consumers. In recent years, there have been many forest fires in the western United States. Suppose a fire burns part of a forest to the ground. What do you think will happen over time? This disaster causes succession to occur in stages.

The first organisms to grow in the burned-out area are grasses and weeds. They are able to grow from seeds left in the soil. What used to be a forest is now a grassy meadow. Insects, reptiles, birds, and small mammals begin to return to the area. The forest has changed to an open field or meadow.

During the next stage, the open field changes as shrubs and small trees begin to grow. The trees and shrubs make shady areas that cause some of the original grasses to die. As more shrubs and small trees grow, the animal populations shift. Larger birds of prey and mammals will come to the area that now provides them with shelter. The grassy field has changed into shrub land.

Over time, as pine trees grow and provide more shade, the shrubs and smaller trees are crowded out. When they die off, what is left is a pine forest. As the pine trees grow, different consumer populations move in. The community of a pine forest is different from that of shrub land or an open field.

Eventually, the fourth stage occurs as hardwood trees begin to grow in the area. As they slowly crowd out the pine trees, a hardwood forest community develops. Again, different plants lead to different consumers, and a new animal community evolves to fit the environment.

Changes in Our Ecosystems (cont.)

Climax Community

Once the hardwood forest develops, succession stops. The hardwood forest is one example of a **climax community**, the last community to form. It will remain virtually unchanged until new environmental changes occur. A climax community usually has diverse (varied) populations of organisms living in it. What a climax community looks like depends on the biome in which it is located. The formation of a climax community is a very slow process, which could take 100 years or more. Natural disasters, such as forest fires, flooding, volcanoes, and earthquakes, can destroy parts of climax communities in a short time. If you see the devastation of a forest fire, you must realize that it will not return to a forest again in your lifetime.

Balancing Act

In a **balanced ecosystem**, the size of a population may go up or down from year to year, but the average size of the population remains the same over time. For example, one year there might be a large amount of mice. As a result, the number of foxes increases. The larger number of foxes eat more of the mice, and the next year, there are fewer mice around. More foxes starve to death. Now that there are fewer foxes, the mice numbers again increase. And so the balance of the ecosystem is maintained. The mouse and fox numbers will change year to year, but remain constant throughout the decades.

Sometimes, the balance of nature gets upset. Just one change in the population of one organism can be harmful to the other organisms that live in the community. While natural forces, such as forest fires, can alter the balance, humans can also upset the balance of nature. Habitat destruction is one way humans have influenced the balance of the environment. We clear cut forests and prairies to create farms, roads, and towns. These actions are permanent and do not allow the environment to return to normal. This makes it hard for some animals and plants to thrive and reproduce. So in our example of the mice and the foxes, let's imagine the meadow where they lived has been cleared to make room for a housing subdivision. Perhaps the mice would move into garages and basements, causing expensive damage to homes. The foxes might die out entirely, because they have no way to hunt the mice that have moved indoors.

Over time, this can lead to a species becoming **threatened**. Threatened means there are fewer of these animals than there used to be. Their population is beginning to drop. If the decline continues, the population will become endangered or even extinct. There are many animals on the list of **endangered** species. Endangered animals, such as the whooping crane, giant panda, and humpback whale, are in danger of becoming **extinct**. When an animal becomes extinct, no more of that animal exist on our planet. While the dinosaurs are a well-known group of extinct animals, other creatures, such as the dodo, have been driven to extinction by humans. The population of people on Earth increased from nearly 7 billion to over 8 billion in just the last 10 years. What do you think will happen if people continue to settle in new areas?

Name: ______________________________ Date: ______________

Changes in Our Ecosystems: Reinforcement Activity

To the student observer: Suppose a pine tree forest burns. Why is it that the pine trees are not the first community in the succession?

____

____

____

Analyze: Is the climax community the same everywhere? Why or why not?

____

____

____

Completion:

1. A process in which a community gradually changes over time when the environment has changed is called ____________________.
2. The last change in a succession is the ____________________.
3. The first populations to change in succession are the ____________________.
4. Succession occurs after natural disasters such as ____________________, ____________________, and ____________________.
5. Open meadows change during succession into ____________________ land.
6. Each time the plant life changes, the ____________________ life changes too.
7. A hardwood forest is one example of a ____________________ community.
8. Sometimes when the environment changes, it is working to maintain a (an) ____________________ ecosystem.
9. ____________________ may also upset the balance of nature by building roads.
10. List below, in order from first to last, the four stages of succession after a forest fire:

    A. ______________________________

    B. ______________________________

    C. ______________________________

    D. ______________________________

The Ozone Layer and the Greenhouse Effect

Close to the Ground

Ozone is a gas in the atmosphere that is a form of oxygen. It consists of three oxygen atoms bonded together in a molecule and is written as O_3. *Ozone* is based on the Greek word meaning "to smell." Can you smell a thunderstorm? The metallic odor produced during the thunderstorm is O_3. Some O_3 forms as lightning passes through the air; other O_3 is made when sunlight reacts with the gases made by plants and microbes in the soil.

Scientists believe there is too much O_3 in the atmosphere. Did you also know that scientists also agree there is too little ozone in the atmosphere? How can that be true? Actually, both are correct. It depends on where the O_3 is in the atmosphere.

The lower atmosphere contains the air we breathe; O_3 close to the ground is generally considered to be bad. One way we have contributed to the problem is the brownish-yellowish haze called **smog**. Smog is created from our cars' exhaust and factories. O_3 in the lower atmosphere makes your eyes water and irritates your nose, throat, and lungs. It increases coughing, headaches, and drowsiness. Next time you get sleepy in class, try blaming it on too much O_3 in the atmosphere! O_3 in the lower atmosphere stunts the growth of plants and reduces flowering. Remember, many flowers are fertilized through pollination, which produces the fruits and vegetables we eat. Could this eventually affect our food supply? This is why some scientists say that too much ozone is a bad thing. If too much O_3 is harmful, why are scientists expressing concern for the possible destruction of the ozone layer?

The Ozone Layer

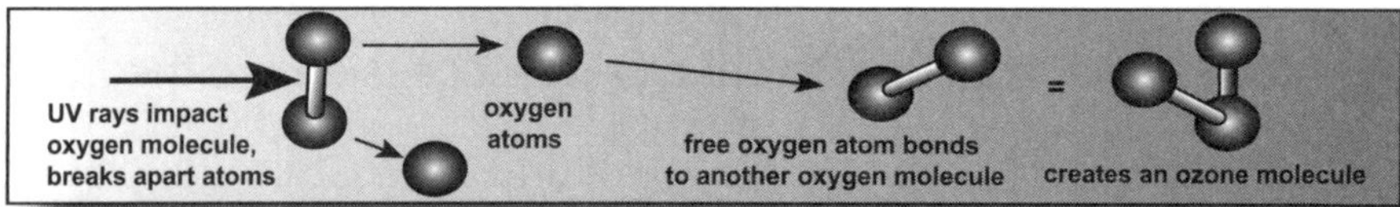

In the **stratosphere**, or upper atmosphere, O_3 is naturally produced and is actually beneficial. It is essential for life on Earth to continue. O_3 is naturally created in the stratosphere when ultraviolet (UV) radiation from the sun comes in contact with oxygen. Approximately 90% of the O_3 gases are found evenly spread in a thin layer throughout the stratosphere. In fact, if all the O_3 in the **stratosphere** (a layer that is over 20 miles thick) were compressed into one layer, it would only be 1/8th of an inch thick! Weird, huh?

While the sun is necessary for life on Earth, it also produces UV radiation, which can cause skin cancer and cataracts and kills tiny ocean creatures called plankton, a major food source for marine animals. The layer of O_3 in the stratosphere blocks harmful UV radiation. Less O_3 allows these harmful rays to reach the earth's surface. That's why scientists say O_3 in the upper atmosphere is good. The problem is a group of chemicals called **chlorofluorocarbons** (CFCs). CFCs in the atmosphere increased beginning in the 1930s when people started using them for various industrial purposes like aerosol sprays, refrigeration units, and polystyrene. These were thought to be responsible for the slow destruction of the ozone layer. When UV rays from the sun and CFCs combine, they break up the O_3 in the upper atmosphere more quickly than it can be reformed naturally. Over time, scientists noticed a decrease in the protective O_3 layer in the stratosphere. A hole in the ozone layer over Antarctica was discovered to be growing at an alarming rate in the 1980s. International action has taken place to decrease the use of CFCs, with almost all of the substances being banned or phased out. Scientists are now seeing a slow recovery of the ozone layer. It may repair itself in about 40 years.

The Ozone Layer and the Greenhouse Effect (cont.)

The Greenhouse Effect

What is the **greenhouse effect**? Many plants are grown in glass buildings called greenhouses that trap heat, making the buildings and plants warmer than the temperature outside. Like a greenhouse, our atmosphere is trapping heat. **Global warming** refers to the warming of the earth's atmosphere, water, and surface temperature. It can be natural or manmade. How is the earth trapping heat? It happens through the production of greenhouse gases. The **greenhouse gases** include water vapor, methane, nitrous oxide, CFCs, and O_3. While water vapor is most abundant, the water cycle ensures that the amount of water vapor remains constant, and it does not contribute to the greenhouse effect. Instead, global warming is the result of the introduction of more of the other greenhouse gases than our planet can absorb. Don't get the wrong idea—without greenhouse gases, Earth would be too cold to support much life. The average temperature would be below freezing. But balance is key. When the right balance of gases exists in the air, they help the planet. But when there are more gases than needed, they can cause harm.

Let's look at carbon dioxide (CO_2) to better understand this balance. CO_2 is vital to life. Plants use it to make food and then release oxygen as waste. Animals breathe oxygen and exhale CO_2 as waste. This exchange maintains a proper balance of CO_2. However, humans have altered the balance. Our cars and machines burn fossil fuels, which increase the amount of CO_2 in the atmosphere. At the same time, cutting down tropical rain forests to clear land for farming has significantly reduced the amount of plants available to change the CO_2 into oxygen. Some ecologists predict that, as a result of the increases in greenhouse gases like CO_2, temperatures will rise, melting the polar ice caps, and sea levels will rise. To help prevent increases in greenhouse gases, we must educate people about reducing carbon dioxide levels by exploring alternative energy sources and becoming more energy efficient.

Changing Climates

Climatic changes could result in more violent storms, floods, and droughts. Higher temperatures could lead to the extinction of some plants and animals. This could result in a loss of food sources and habitats for many animal species. Major food crops like rice, wheat, and corn might not be able to grow in the areas they do today, which would have a negative economical impact in many areas. Remember, even if people greatly reduce emissions, greenhouse gases remain in the atmosphere for a long time, and the climate could be affected for many years to come. Have you seen any evidence that suggests these things are already happening?

What Can We Do?

Burning fossil fuels for energy is the greatest source of greenhouse gases. Fossil fuels include energy sources such as coal, gasoline, and natural gas. By finding new sources of energy, we can help reduce greenhouse gases. Solar power is an energy source that doesn't produce greenhouse gases. Cars that run on hydrogen are also being developed as an alternative to gasoline.

Name: ______________________________ Date: ______________

The Ozone Layer and the Greenhouse Effect: Reinforcement Activity

To the student observer: Do you see evidence that suggests that some of the events discussed in the lesson have already begun? Explain.

Analyze: How has the decrease in CFCs affected the ozone layer? What does that say about the effect people can have on the environment?

Review:

1. What is the ozone layer? Why is it important?
2. What causes ozone to form naturally in the upper atmosphere? Lower atmosphere?
3. Explain why scientists say the earth has too little AND too much ozone.
4. What chemicals were destroying the ozone layer? Where was this destruction most visible?
5. What is causing the temperature of the earth to increase? What is this called?
6. Name the greenhouse gases.
7. What are some ways humans have contributed to the greenhouse effect?
8. List two concerns experts have regarding global warming.

Think About It:

How much do you contribute to the greenhouse effect? What are some things you could do to reduce the amount of greenhouse gases you generate?

Learning About Pollution

Pollution

Ever since humankind first gathered together in settlements, there has been pollution. **Pollution** is a term used to describe the release of harmful materials into the environment. By making our lives better and more comfortable, we unknowingly have created an imbalance in the natural world. We created waste that nature could not break down and reuse. We produced **non-biodegradable** things that would not decompose and return into the natural cycles. We have disturbed these cycles or upset the balance of nature by producing more or less of a natural substance. Technology and soaring world population have changed the balance between man's demands and the earth's capacity for meeting them. We not only take more from the earth than is replaced; we misuse much of it. We have allowed our waste to contaminate the air, water, and soil. How do we learn to change our behavior to prevent further damage?

Air Pollution

Air is all around us. We cannot see it, but we can see the effects of wind (moving air) when a tree sways, a kite flies, or a sailboat moves across the water. Air is a mixture of several gases: nitrogen (78%), oxygen (21%), and argon (1%). Carbon dioxide, neon, helium, methane, and other gases exist in trace amounts in the air we breathe.

Air pollution is the contamination of air by the discharge of harmful substances. It causes many health problems for people, especially the young, the elderly, and those with respiratory problems. These problems include burning eyes and noses, irritated throats, and difficulty in breathing. Some of the chemicals found in polluted air can cause cancer, birth defects, brain and nerve damage, and long-term injury to our lungs. Air pollution also causes damage to the environment and property by eroding stone and wood and weakening metal. This in turn wears down our homes, roads, and bridges. It also affects plants and trees, stunting their growth or killing them. It affects the health of our rivers, lakes, and streams and all the plants and animals that depend on these water sources. Air pollution has been elevated to a global concern because of four developments: increased traffic, growing cities, rapid economic development, and industrialization.

The problem of air pollution will not be resolved easily or quickly. Governments, industries, and individuals throughout the world must work together to solve this problem by setting reasonable controls on emissions from factories and vehicles while monitoring the environment.

Sulfuric and nitric acids form in the upper atmosphere.

Learning About Pollution (cont.)

Acid Rain

Acid rain forms in the atmosphere because of air pollution. Rain becomes acidic when gases dissolve in water vapor. When factories and power plants burn fossil fuels, sulfur and nitrogen oxides are released. Automobile exhaust also releases nitrogen oxide. These gases rise into the atmosphere, where they combine with water vapor to form sulfuric and nitric acids. The polluted water vapor falls back to earth as acid rain. The acid rain soaks into the soil, where it can stunt plant growth and damage leaves. When it falls into lakes and rivers, it kills fish and aquatic plants. As rain falls back to Earth, it causes both land and water pollution. Since rain falls far from where it is formed, acid rain is a global problem that should concern us all. It can take years for an acidic lake or stream to recover from this type of pollution.

Acid rain is a term used to describe rain with a pH below 5. Acidity is measured using a scale called the **pH scale**. It goes from 0 to 14. Anything with a pH level of 7 is considered to be **neutral**. A number above 7 is **alkaline**—the higher a number is above 7, the more alkaline a substance. A number below 7 is **acidic**—the lower the number below seven, the more acidic it is (acidic means containing acid). The pH scale is logarithmic. Each number is 10 times the amount of the previous number.

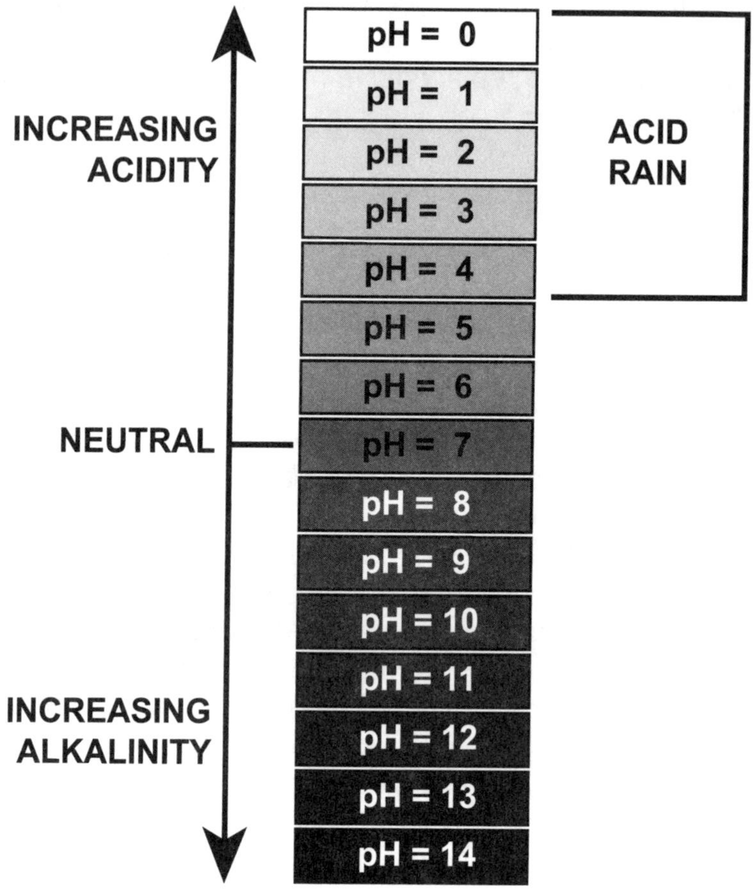

Name: ______________________________ Date: ______________

Learning About Pollution: Reinforcement Activity

To the student observer: Who or what is at the most risk from acid rain or air pollution? Why do you think that? Provide examples to support your claim.

____

____

____

Analyze: Are you partially responsible for acid rain? Why or why not?

____

____

____

Completion:

1. ____________________ is the release of harmful materials into the environment.
2. Air pollution causes ____________________ problems in humans.
3. Air pollution causes damage to the ____________________ and ____________________.
4. Air is a mixture of different ____________________.
5. ____________________ ____________________ forms in the atmosphere because of air pollution.
6. Acid rain falls back to earth, causing ____________________ and water pollution.
7. Acid rain has a ____________________ level below 5.
8. ____________________ is measured by using a pH scale.
9. A pH number of 7 is considered to be ____________________.
10. A pH number above 7 is considered to be ____________________.

Think About It:
How are problems with global warming connected to problems with air pollution?

____

____

____

Keeping the Planet Healthy

The Hydrosphere

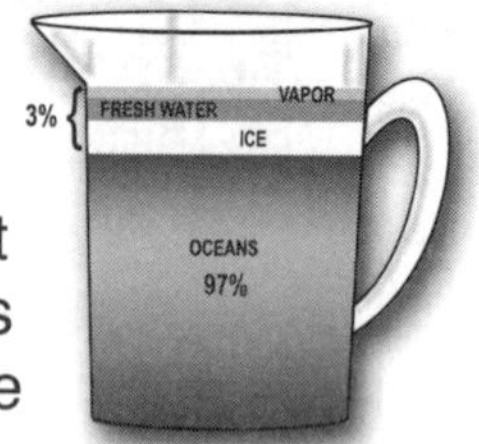

We have learned about the effects of pollution on the air we breathe and the water we drink. Since all living things need water to maintain good health, it is a good idea to understand the **hydrosphere**. The hydrosphere is the part of the earth's biosphere that contains all the water on our planet. Water moves continuously through the hydrosphere in a cycle. Fortunately, most of us realize water is one of our most valued resources. Unfortunately, 97% of the water on Earth is salt water. If you do the math, this leaves us with only 3% freshwater. However, 2% of the freshwater on Earth is unavailable; it is trapped inside glaciers, ice caps, and mountain snow. The remaining 1% of water on our planet that is available for us to use is stored in the soil or in our lakes and rivers. This is why it is so important for us to conserve water and keep it unpolluted.

Freshwater Pollution

Our rivers, lakes, and streams are often polluted by factories. Factories use large amounts of water that become contaminated with poisonous chemicals during manufacturing processes. If this water leaks into our water supply, it becomes polluted. Farmers use fertilizers and other chemicals to help their plants grow and keep insect pests away. If these chemicals, as well as the waste from the herds of animals, enter the water supply, it causes a type of green algae to grow at a rapid rate. When this algae grows rapidly, it is called **blooming**. This rapid growth quickly uses up all the available oxygen in the water. These blooms of algae can take over a lake and kill all the fish and other aquatic organisms that live there.

Other problems include waste water from our sinks, tubs, washing machines, and toilets. If untreated waste water enters our lakes and rivers, the pollution can kill the organisms that call the freshwater area home. Many of the products we use in our daily lives contain chemicals that are harmful. When these products, such as paints, insect sprays, hair products, and old batteries, end up piled in dumps, the rainwater can carry the chemicals down into the soil and into the groundwater.

Ocean Water Pollution

When you look at a globe, you can easily see how the surface of our planet is mostly oceans. They are all connected and really a part of one big body of water. Even though we don't drink or use the ocean waters for agricultural purposes, ocean pollution is still a concern. The oceans' many living things provide us with food and medicines, and the waters provide minerals, such as salt and manganese.

Some people used to believe that the oceans were so big that dumping waste into them wouldn't matter. Today, we know better. Garbage dumped into the ocean contaminates beaches and spreads disease-causing germs. Chemicals dumped in the oceans, either on purpose or by accident, slowly work through the food chain. If plankton, a common food for primary consumers, take in the poisonous chemicals, it is passed on through the food chain to the second- and third-level consumer fish. People who eat fish may be eating pollution. There are laws that prohibit the dumping of poisonous chemicals directly into our rivers, lakes, and oceans, but we must be careful to prevent accidental contaminations as well.

Keeping the Planet Healthy (cont.)

Land Pollution

You have learned about pollution and how it effects the air we breathe and the water we drink. You have explored the effects of pollution on the atmosphere and the hydrosphere. All the pollution you've learned about is from the lithosphere. The **lithosphere** is the land upon which people live, and, unfortunately, it is where pollution begins.

Soil is the top layer of the earth's crust. It is a very thin layer that is filled with an immense variety of organisms, such as bacterium and other microorganisms, which help maintain the ecological balance of the environment. These organisms break down dead plants and animals into their building blocks so that the nutrients can be reused by other plants and animals. This is the circle of life at the most basic level.

Only a very small portion of the earth, about 21%, is suitable for farming. The other 79% is too shallow, too dry, too cold, too wet, or too poor in nutrients to be used for farming. While modern farmers have tried chemical shortcuts to boost the nutrients in the soil, as we learned earlier, the runoff can lead to water pollution.

Land pollution is also caused by hazardous chemicals from factories and mines. Many factories use poisonous chemicals in the production of everything from gasoline to athletic shoes. Gold mining releases cyanide, which is a deadly gas that poisons the soil. Other types of mining use chemicals to break down and separate the minerals. Dumps allow chemicals from cars, computers, and appliances to seep into the soil. All of these forms of pollution destroy the vital organisms that keep the soil healthy. Even though you cannot see the microorganisms that live in the soil, your health and well-being are directly connected to theirs.

Healthy Solutions

If we could get people to do a few very simple things every day, it could improve the health of our planet tomorrow and in the future. Most people know about **recycling**. Recycling reuses materials, which saves raw materials. Think of all the trees we save by using recycled paper products and cardboard. Recycling also reduces the amount of energy consumed to make new products. The United States uses over 100 million steel cans every day. Recycling those cans means less mining and less energy spent making raw steel into new cans. The same is true of plastic, aluminum, and glass containers.

Reuse is another way to reduce pollution. Think of ways you can reuse empty containers around the house. Even something as simple as using a milk jug as a watering can helps the environment. Another way to recycle and reuse is composting. **Compost** is what happens naturally to dead plant matter. Think of a forest. Every year, the trees shed lots of leaves, but the forest is never buried in leaves. Instead, the leaves are broken down by microorganisms and turned into nutrient-rich dirt, which leads to healthier trees. The leaves are composted. You can do the same thing with your yard waste and kitchen scraps. By composting, you reduce the amount of material dumped in landfills. You also get rich, healthy soil for a better lawn and garden!

Name: ______________________________ Date: ______________

Keeping the Planet Healthy: Reinforcement Activity

To the student observer: Do you think land pollution is a serious problem? Why or why not?

Analyze: Why do you think some people evade the laws and illegally dump harmful waste?

True or False: Read each statement below and decide if you agree (T) or disagree (F) with the statement.

____ 1. Most of the earth's surface is land.

____ 2. The hydrosphere is the part of the earth's biosphere that contains all the water on our planet.

____ 3. Approximately 97% of the water on Earth is saltwater.

____ 4. Blooms of algae reduce pollution in ponds.

____ 5. Only 1% of water on our planet is available for us to use.

____ 6. Oceans are so large that dumping waste into them doesn't matter.

____ 7. Most of the land (97%) on earth is suitable for farming and crop production.

____ 8. Land pollution is caused by hazardous chemicals from factories, farms, and mining operations.

____ 9. The soil has become polluted when it is full of bacteria and other microorganisms.

____ 10. Healthy solutions for our planet include recycling/reusing materials, composting yard waste, and not littering our neighborhoods.

Think About It: Gather information about the problem below and develop a solution.

Much of the garbage we produce is from the "overpackaging" of products we buy. Do you think this is a problem? Do you have any solutions?

Research Activity: Alternatives to Fossil Fuels

To the student observer: Energy is vital for our basic needs, like heating our homes, cooking our food, and getting from place to place. Most of the energy we use today comes from the burning of fossil fuels. Since industrialization, the burning of fossil fuels has greatly increased the amount of carbon dioxide in the atmosphere. You have learned that carbon dioxide in the atmosphere plays an important role in warming the earth by trapping the sun's heat in what is called the greenhouse effect. Experts warn that, if allowed to continue, the greenhouse effect could lead to global warming, which could have disastrous outcomes for the planet's environments and people. To keep the level of carbon dioxide in check, we must find alternative forms of energy and become more energy efficient. We must carefully choose the sources of energy we use, because the choices we make today will determine our environment in the future.

Research Activity: Below is a list of alternative forms of energy. Investigate at least two of these. Be sure to answer the questions in the "Think It Over" section for each form of energy. Decide which energy source is best for our planet and share what you have learned.

Alternative forms of energy:

Solar collectors	Gasohol	Hydroelectric power
Methane	Windmills	Nuclear power plants
Ethanol	Biodiesel	Passive solar energy

Think It Over:

1. How does this energy source work?
2. From where does this form of energy come?
3. From what is this energy source made?
4. How efficient is this form of energy?
5. What are the advantages and the disadvantages of this energy source?
6. Why should people use this form of energy?

Ecology: Vocabulary

abiotic: the nonliving factors of an environment
air pollution: the contamination of air by the discharge of harmful substances
acid rain: a harmful rain that is caused by pollution and has a low pH level
balanced ecosystem: the size of the population may go up or down from year to year, but the average size of the population remains the same
biome: an ecosystem found over a large geographic area
biotic: the living parts of an environment
biosphere: the part of the earth where living things can exist
blooming: when algae grows rapidly due to an increase in chemicals in the water
carnivore: consumer that eats other animals
carrying capacity: largest amount of a population that can be supported by an area
chlorofluorocarbons (CFCs): a group of chemicals used in aerosal sprays, refrigeration units, and polystyrene that are thought to be responsible for the slow destruction of the ozone layer
climate: the weather in an area over a long period of time
climax community: the last community to form in the process of succession
commensalism: a relationship in which one organism benefits and the other is unaffected
community: a group of different populations that live in the same area
compost: dead plant matter that is broken down by microorganisms and turned into nutrient-rich dirt
condensation: when water vapor in the air cools and changes into liquid water droplets
consumer: an organism that gets its food by eating, or consuming, other organisms
cycle: something that happens over and over again in the same way
decomposer: organism that gets its food by breaking down complex chemicals in dead organisms into simple chemicals that become part of the soil
ecology: study of interactions among living things and the nonliving things in their environment
ecosystem: the interactions among the populations of a community and the nonliving things in their environment
endangered: when there are almost no animals or plants left of a certain species
environment: everything that surrounds an organism
estuaries: areas where salt water and fresh water mix
evaporation: when liquid water changes to the gas water vapor and rises from oceans, rivers, and lakes to become part of the air
extinct: when all members of a certain species are dead
first-order consumer: eats plants
food chain: the feeding order of organisms in a community
food web: all the food chains in a community that are linked together
fossil fuels: fuels formed long ago from the remains of plants and animals
global warming: the gradual warming of the earth's atmosphere, water, and surface temperature
greenhouse gases: water vapor, methane, nitrous oxide, CFCs, ozone, and other gases that prevent heat from escaping the earth's atmosphere
groundwater: water just beneath the surface of the land
habitat: the natural home of an organism

Ecology: Vocabulary (cont.)

herbivore: consumer that eats only plants
hydrosphere: the part of earth's biosphere that contains all the water on the planet
interact: to act upon or influence something
limiting factors: conditions in the environment that put limits on where an organism can live
lithosphere: the land upon which people live; the surface of the earth
mutualism: a relationship in which both organisms benefit
niches: roles organisms play in their environments
nitrogen-fixing bacteria: change nitrogen gas into nitrogen compounds, or nitrates
nocturnal: only active at night
non-biodegradable: things that do not decompose and return into natural cycles
nonnative species: a new species introduced into an environment
nonrenewable resources: the things that cannot be naturally replaced
nutrients: substances that organisms use for growth, repair, and energy
omnivore: consumer that eats both plants and animals
organism: living thing
ozone (O_3): a gas that is a form of oxygen in the atmosphere consisting of three oxygen atoms bonded together
parasitism: a relationship in which one organism benefits and the other organism is harmed
permafrost: permanently frozen ground
photosynthesis: the process where producers use sunlight to make their food; plants take in carbon dioxide to make food and give off oxygen as a waste product
pollution: something added to the environment that is harmful to living things
population: a group of organisms of the same species that live in the same area
precipitation: water that falls to earth from clouds in the form of rain, snow, sleet, or hail
predator: an animal that hunts another animal for food
producer: an organism that can capture the energy from the sun to make its own food
prey: an animal that is hunted
range: the area where a type of animal or plant population is found
recycling: reusing materials
renewable resource: the things that are replaced by nature
resource: anything that an organism uses to live
respiration: animals take in oxygen and give off carbon dioxide as waste
second-order consumer: eats animals that eat plants
smog: fog or haze combined with smoke and other pollutants in the air
soil: the top layer of the earth's crust; a thin layer filled with organisms such as bacteria and other microorganisms
succession: the process by which a community changes over time
symbiosis: relationships between two organisms
third-order consumer: eats animals that eat other animals
threatened: when there are fewer of a species of animal or plant than there used to be
trade-off: giving up one thing in favor of another
water vapor: the gas form of water present in the air

Ecology Projects

To the student observer: Here are some enjoyable projects to help you learn more about ecology.

Project: Build and Study an Ant Colony

Materials Needed:

- 3 pieces of wood (12″ x 1″)
- Cheesecloth
- Strong elastic band
- 2 pieces of clear plastic (12″ square)
- Hammer and nails
- Garden soil/sand/leaf litter
- Glue
- Colony of ants

What To Do:

1. Fasten the three wood pieces into the shape of a square missing its top. Place glue all around the edge of the frame on one side. Attach a piece of the plastic to the frame. Turn the frame over and repeat. Leave this to dry for a couple of days.
2. Once dry, fill the frame to about six inches from the top with alternating layers of sand and soil (so that the tunnels and chambers will show). Top it off with a thin layer of leaf litter. Be sure to leave about a 5-inch gap at the top to give the ants some space.
3. Collect some ants (look under large stones). Use a soft brush and a jar to collect the ants. Try to find a larger queen ant to include. Empty the ants into their new home. Give them some water (a moist cotton ball will do) and some sugar, an apple, or other food scraps. Secure the observatory by placing the cheesecloth over the top and using the elastic band to hold it in place. Now enjoy watching the ants work! Look for the different niches they fill in the colony. Look for ants that guard the colony, search for food, tend to the young, or look after the queen. Watch as they build complex passageways. Identify which foods they prefer by leaving them different sorts of food. Study the different stages in their life cycle.

Project: Make Recycled Paper

Materials Needed:

- Old newspapers
- 2 buckets or large bowls
- Spoon or blender
- Wire mesh (found in hardware or garden centers)
- Powder paint (to make colored paper)
- Weights or heavy books
- Cloth towels
- Plastic bags

What To Do:

1. Place newspaper in a bucket and add enough water to completely cover the paper. Soak the old newspapers in the bucket overnight.
2. The next day, drain off any extra water and then use the spoon or blender to mash up the paper and water into a pulp. Be sure to clean the blender afterwards.
3. Mix in the paint if you want colored paper.
4. Put the pulp into the bucket and add an equal amount of water. Mix these together. Slide the wire mesh into the mixture, making sure to get it covered in pulp. Lift it out carefully.
5. Lay the cloth on a flat surface. Place the mesh pulp-side down quickly and carefully onto the cloth. Press down hard and peel the mesh off, leaving the pulp behind on the cloth. Put another cloth on top and press down firmly. Repeat these steps with your remaining pulp and cloths. When this is done, place the plastic bag on the top and weight the pile down.
6. After several hours, the pulp should turn to paper. Gently peel the paper off the cloths. Lay them on some newspaper to finish drying. The paper should now be ready to use.

Ecology Projects

Project: Build a Mini-Greenhouse

Materials Needed:

Clear containers with lids
Seeds or small plants
Potting soil

What To Do:

1. Put the potting soil about two inches deep in the bottom of your greenhouse containers and add a few small plants or seeds. Water thoroughly and close the lid. Place your greenhouses in a sunny location.
2. Observe the conditions inside your greenhouse every day for at least two weeks. Keep a log describing the conditions in the greenhouses and illustrate the growth of the plants.
3. After two weeks, compare the various greenhouses. Which one produced the most plant growth? Which produced the least plant growth? Why do you think that happened?

Project: Build a Compost Heap

Materials Needed:

Organic waste from the kitchen (no meat scraps)
Some soil
Grass clippings or leaves
Zip ties
Water
Chicken wire (about three yards, available at most hardware stores)
Piece of old carpet or plastic sheeting

What To Do:

1. Find a spot (about 1½ square yards in size) and make a barrel shape with the wire. Use the zip ties to secure the wire.
2. The bottom layer should be twigs and sticks. Then alternate layers of yard waste, kitchen waste, and soil. Add water to keep the layers moist and pack layers down firmly.
3. When the heap is about two feet high, lay the old carpet or plastic sheeting over the top to keep the heat in. About once a month, turn your compost with a shovel to make sure enough air gets to the center. After five or six months, you will have compost.

Project: Make Your Own Water Cycle

Materials Needed:

Large bowl
Smaller plastic bowl
Small weight
Plastic wrap

What To Do:

1. Put water into the large bowl and place it in the sun.
2. Put a small bowl inside the large bowl. It will float on the water in the large bowl.
3. Cover the large bowl with plastic wrap and put the small weight on top of the plastic wrap, directly over the small bowl. The heat evaporates the water, which rises and condenses on the cool plastic, only to fall back into the small bowl inside the container.

Name: ______________________________ Date: ________________

Ecology Unit Test

Multiple Choice:

1. Everything that surrounds a living thing makes up its
   a. population. b. environment. c. niche. d. range.

2. Ecology is the study of the environment and
   a. living things. b. water. c. soil. d. air.

3. All of one kind of organism that lives in a certain place make up a/an
   a. population. b. community. c. ecosystem. d. environment.

4. The organism's role or job in its habitat is its
   a. environment. b. limiting factor. c. range. d. niche.

5. All the populations that live in a certain area make up a/an
   a. community. b. niche. c. ecosystem. d. range.

6. The limiting factors of a population determine its
   a. range. b. cycle. c. niche. d. ecosystem.

7. Plants in the environment are called
   a. consumers. b. decomposers. c. producers. d. scavengers.

8. Evergreens are plants that cover most of the area in a __________ biome.
   a. coniferous forest b. desert c. deciduous forest d. rain forest

9. A food web shows the relationship between
   a. renewable resources. b. natural resources.
   c. food chains. d. energy pyramids.

10. All of the following cycle in the environment except
    a. rocks. b. people. c. nitrogen. d. carbon dioxide.

11. An example of a nonrenewable resource is
    a. water. b. natural gas. c. soil. d. air.

12. An example of a renewable resource is
    a. wind. b. oil. c. coal. d. natural gas.

13. The biome where the ground is permanently frozen is the
    a. coniferous forest. b. desert. c. tundra. d. deciduous forest.

14. A relationship in which both organisms benefit is called
    a. commensalism. b. parasitism. c. mutualism. d. competition.

Name: ______________________ Date: ____________

Ecology Unit Test (cont.)

15. Oxygen and carbon dioxide are cycled through the environment by the process of respiration and
    a. photosynthesis. b. evaporation. c. the water cycle. d. the nitrogen cycle.

16. The word *ecosystem* refers to:
    a. the physical environment
    b. living organisms
    c. both a and b
    d. none of the above

17. Which statement below is true?
    a. You can always predict what will happen when you introduce a new species to the wild.
    b. New species will always add to the biodiversity of an area.
    c. both a and b
    d. none of the above

18. Which of the following photosynthesize?
    a. producers b. decomposers c. consumers d. none of the above

19. A food web shows the flow of __________ through the ecosystem.
    a. populations b. energy c. consumers d. none of the above

20. Which of the following factors could affect carrying capacity?
    a. amount of food available
    b. competition for living space
    c. climate change
    d. all of the above.

21. Imagine that a population has reached its carrying capacity. A competing species enters the area. The carrying capacity for the original population is likely to:
    a. increase.
    b. decrease.
    c. stay the same.
    d. increase, then decrease.

22. When water evaporates, it changes into
    a. liquid. b. a solid. c. a gaseous vapor. d. the lithosphere.

23. An animal that hunts other animals for food is a
    a. predator b. stalker c. prey d. producer

Short Answer:

24. Do you contribute to the condition known as acid rain? Why or why not?

____

____

____

Answer Keys

What Is Ecology? (pg. 3)

To the student observer: Accept all logical answers.
Negative effects: Pollution—air, land, or water (litter, exhaust fumes by driving cars)
Positive effects: Ride your bike or walk more, plant some trees, recycle and reuse trash
Analyze: Accept all logical answers—school, swimming pool, camping, home, neighborhood, the city park
Completion:
1. ecology 2. environment 3. materials
4. plants 5. carbon dioxide 6. nutrients
7. interact 8. biotic 9. abiotic
10. biosphere 11. habitat 12. community

Think About It: (in any order)
1. water 2. oxygen 3. carbon dioxide
4. nutrients 5. energy

What Is an Ecosystem? (pg. 6)

To the student observer: Answers will vary but should indicate a forest community.
Analyze: Answers will vary.
Largest: microorganisms
Smallest: top predators like wolves
Other: elk, trees, mice, birds, etc.
Completion:
1. community 2. ecosystem 3. sun
4. decomposes (decays) 5. habitat
6. niche 7. habitat, niche
8. a. production of energy (sunlight)
   b. energy must be stored or transferred
   c. dead things break down or decay into raw materials
   d. raw materials are returned to the soil or reused

Making an Inference: No, it has a thick coat of fur. It is "well suited" for life in the cold arctic region. It would not be able to survive in the desert heat.

Learning About the Web of Life (pg. 9)

To the student observer: Consumers eat other organisms—they obtain their food from outside their body. Producers have the ability to convert the sun's energy into food—they make their own food inside special cell structures in a process called photosynthesis.
Analyze: omnivore—eating meat and cheese that come from animals, and lettuce, tomato, onions, pickles, and grains from plants.
Completion:
1. sun 2. producer 3. Decomposers
4. Algae 5. first 6. eating

Identify:
1. C 2. B 3. A 4. A 5. C 6. B

Prove You Can:
1. Answers will vary. Third-order or top level is the smallest—the energy has decreased as it flows through the food chain.
2. A food web is a combination of many food chains within the community. Several food chains make a food web.
3. Some of it (the original source of energy) has been used up by the organism (carrying out life processes) or it has escaped as heat before that organism is consumed by the next order consumer. Each time it is passed from one level or order consumer to the next order, the amount of the sun's original energy decreases.
4. They feed on dead organisms (cleaning our environment) and enrich the soil by returning the nutrients. They are responsible for recycling raw materials to be used over and over again by plants and animals.

Symbiosis (pg. 10)

Answers will vary.

Predator and Prey Adaptations (pg. 11)

Answers will vary.

Round and Round We Go: Cycles in the Ecosystem (pg. 14)

To the student observer: Water, carbon, oxygen, and nitrogen (students may suggest rock)
Analyze: Over time we might use up these needed substances
Completion:
1. photosynthesis 2. proteins 3. Bacteria
4. materials 5. oxygen
6. liquid, evaporating 7. Oxygen/Carbon dioxide
8. carbon dioxide 9. plants

Predict: The oxygen content would begin to decrease.
Name That Cycle:
a. nitrogen b. carbon dioxide/oxygen c. water

Answer Keys (cont.)

What are Biomes? (pg. 18)
To the student observer: A biome is a large region on earth with its own unique climate, plants, animals, and soil.
Analyze: Answers will vary.
Identify:
1. Tundra 2. Desert 3. Tropical Rain Forest
4. Grasslands 5. Saltwater (ocean)

Compare/Contrast: Answers will vary; accept all logical answers.

Lake Victoria and the Miracle Fish: Introduction of a New Species (pg. 21)
To the student observer: Answers will vary.
Analyze: Answers will vary.
Thinking It Over:
1. It went from 100,000 to 500,000 metric tons a year. It increased by 400,000 metric tons a year.
2. Student graphs should show an increase in the Nile perch and then a leveling off and possible decine for the future. The total fish will drop off first, and then it will match the Nile perch line, as the other fish disappear. (In reality, the Nile perch have declined since 1995 somewhat due to overfishing, and the other fish have shown some increases.)
3. It provided for the people economically by giving them more to eat and sell. It reduced the number of other fish, and the increase in algae reduced the oxygen level.

Opinion:
Yes point of view: Evidence: 1. More food and money for the people (increased five-fold); 2. Increased jobs by 1993 (16,000 to 82,000); Trade-off: loss of species and creation of dead zones
No point of view: Evidence: 1. Decreased the other fish: may have led to the extinction of 200 species of cichlids; 2. Caused dead zones by depleting oxygen level; Trade-off: less food and fewer jobs if Nile perch not introduced
Teacher note: You may want to show the video "Impact of Invasive Species" by National Geographic to show the impact of the Nile perch in Lake Victoria. The video is at <https://education.nationalgeographic.org/resource/impact-invasive-species>.

Is There Room for One More?: Carrying Capacity (pg. 23–24)
*This assignment challenges students to think about data collected and apply their knowledge.
Think It Over:
1. 4,000 per square meter
2. The numbers are no longer increasing, indicating carrying capacity has been reached.
3. Student answers might reflect on things such as pollution, quality of the water, and competition for food with other species.
4. 2,000 per square meter
5. Student answers might reflect things such as (nonliving) human-induced pollution aspects, temperature change, pH level increased or decreased, amount of precipitation. (Living) food source availability (declined), predators—new species introduced into the lake.
6. Answers will vary.
7. The factory produced pollution that affected either the food source or the mussels.
8. Answers will vary.

Changes in Our Ecosystems (pg. 27)
To the student observer: Grasses are the first plants to reestablish after a fire. Grass seeds survive the fire and grow quickly.
Analyze: No, there are many kinds of communities, depending on where the community is located.
Completion:
1. succession 2. climax community 3. plants
4. fires, floods, volcanoes, earthquakes (any three)
5. shrub 6. animal 7. climax
8. balanced 9. Humans
10. A. Grasslands/Meadows
    B. Shrubs/Shrub land
    C. Pine trees/Pine forest
    D. Hardwood trees/Hardwood forests

The Ozone Layer and the Greenhouse Effect (pg. 30)
To the student observer: Answers will vary—evidence may include statements like "less winter in some areas," "more intense storms in areas—flooding, hurricanes such as Katrina," "drought in many areas—forest fires have increased," "global warming," "increase in the temperature for ocean waters," " research indicating the intense sunlight today is more damaging—more skin

Answer Keys (cont.)

cancer cases," "more people are having respiratory problems—more asthma cases," "more smog and pollution in cities," "studies are finding gene mutations in certain shallow-water animals like frogs," and "the hole found over Antarctica."

Analyze: The ozone layer is repairing itself and it may be repaired in 40 years. The actions of people worldwide can affect the environment and reverse climate change.

Review:

1. A region in the upper atmosphere (stratosphere) that contains 90% of the ozone present; it protects us from UV radiation
2. It forms naturally in the upper atmosphere when UV rays come into contact with oxygen—this is a good thing. In the lower atmosphere, exhaust fumes and lightning react with gases made by plants and microbes in the soil—this is a bad thing. It causes respiratory problems.
3. There is too much O_3 in the lower atmosphere (pollution) and not enough in the upper atmosphere (to protect us from UV radiation).
4. CFCs; above Antarctica
5. increased amount of carbon dioxide from fossil fuels; greenhouse effect (gases)
6. water vapor, methane, nitrous oxide, CFCs, and ozone
7. using fossil fuels such as coal, gasoline, and natural gas; driving cars; cutting forests
8. more violent storms, melting polar ice caps, rising sea levels, and loss of food supply and habitats (any two)

Think About It: Answers will vary.

Learning About Pollution (pg. 33)

To the student observer: Answers will vary. Answers may focus on plants or aquatic animals as being in the most danger. May also focus on the harmful effects on young people, old people, and people with lung problems.

Analyze: Answers will vary.

Completion:

1. Pollution 2. health
3. environment, property 4. gases
5. Acid rain 6. land 7. pH
8. Acidity 9. neutral 10. alkaline

Think About It: Answers will vary. Accept reasonable answers.

Keeping the Planet Healthy (pg. 36)

To the student observer: Answers may vary, but students should understand we depend on the land for many things, such as food and energy needs. If the land is healthy, the plants will be healthy and so will the animals that eat the plants.

Analyze: Answers will vary but may reflect on these ideas—people are lazy, they don't care or believe it really effects them, it costs less.

True or False:

1. F 2. T 3. T 4. F 5. T
6. F 7. F 8. T 9. F 10. T

Think About It: Answers will vary. Students may suggest using biodegradable or recyclable packaging.

Ecology Unit Test (pg. 42–43)

1. b 2. a 3. a 4. d 5. a 6. a
7. c 8. a 9. c 10. b 11. b 12. a
13. c 14. c 15. a 16. c 17. d 18. a
19. b 20. d 21. b 22. c 23. a

Short answer:

24. Answers will vary. Look for supporting ideas, such as using energy created by fossil fuels, burning trash, and buying things made in factories that pollute.